THE
FUNNIEST
FOOTBALL
QUOTES...
EVER!

Also available

The Funniest Liverpool Quotes... Ever!
The Funniest Chelsea Quotes... Ever!
The Funniest West Ham Quotes... Ever!
The Funniest Spurs Quotes... Ever!
The Funniest Arsenal Quotes... Ever!
The Funniest Man City Quotes... Ever!
The Funniest Newcastle Quotes... Ever!
The Funniest United Quotes... Ever!
The Funniest Leeds Quotes... Ever!
The Funniest Boro Quotes... Ever!
The Funniest Forest Quotes... Ever!
The Funniest Sunderland Quotes... Ever!
The Funniest Leicester Quotes... Ever!
The Funniest Saints Quotes... Ever!
The Funniest Everton Quotes... Ever!
The Funniest Villa Quotes... Ever!
The Funniest QPR Quotes... Ever!
The Funniest Celtic Quotes... Ever!
The Funniest Rangers Quotes... Ever!

"I'm sure people will always say he's that idiot who missed that penalty."

THE FUNNIEST ENGLAND QUOTES... EVER!

"It would have been great to win 1-0, but 0-0 seems even better."

by Gordon Law

Printed in Europe and the USA

ISBN: 9798571110716
Imprint: Independently published

Photos courtesy of: Ramzi Musallam and Michael Hulf

Contents

THE FUNNIEST FOOTBALL QUOTES... EVER!

CAN YOU MANAGE?

"I have a number of alternatives and each one gives me something different."
Chelsea manager Glenn Hoddle

"If I was the invisible man for a day, I'd hang around the QPR dressing room to hear what the players say about me."
Harry Redknapp

"I didn't want to talk to people for three weeks after the defeat. I touched my wife but didn't speak to her."
Martin Jol after a Spurs loss

"If I have to move on from Newcastle, hopefully it will be to somewhere else."
Joe Kinnear

"The Championship is a hard league and you're playing against different opposition every week."
Leeds boss Neil Warnock

"Being manager of this club is like wheeling a trolley round Sainsbury's. You want it to go one way, the trolley wants to go the other."
Crystal Palace manager Alan Smith

THE FUNNIEST FOOTBALL QUOTES... EVER!

"Every defeat hurts. You might think it doesn't, but you ask the family. You ask the dog."

Middlesbrough boss Steve McClaren

"My advice to the next England manager? Don't lose matches."

Graham Taylor

"If you can't stand the heat in the dressing room, get out of the kitchen."

Terry Venables

"I believe I could sell a fridge to an Eskimo."

Palace manager Ian Holloway

Can You Manage?

"I want to get more players through the door while the window is open."
Manchester City boss Mark Hughes

"I wouldn't quote Kipling to the lads. They'd probably think I was talking about cakes."
Leicester manager Rob Kelly

"Even the chef's been out for two weeks with a hernia."
West Ham's Alan Curbishley

"I'm like a dog with two dicks."
Joe Royle after an Everton victory

"I could be like the nice uncle, but only if we are winning. Everyone has an uncle they don't like, don't they?"

Ireland assistant manager Roy Keane

"If we do go down it will be just like the day I found out Father Christmas was really my dad."

Leicester boss Micky Adams

"When an Italian tells me it's pasta on the plate I check under the sauce to make sure."

Sir Alex Ferguson

Can You Manage?

"I have often likened a football manager's life to that of a pimp. You depend on other people for your success and are not in control."
Palace boss Steve Coppell

"Yee-ha! I've looked like I've had a coat hanger in my mouth ever since."
Mick McCarthy on being appointed Sunderland manager

"I am supposed to take the bullets and absorb them. Like a bear. A polar bear."
Arsene Wenger on criticism from the fans

"My players say I look like Pete Burns but I don't know who he is. All I know is he's obviously not blessed with good looks."
Palace manager Iain Dowie

"The fans wanted Ginger Spice in basque and suspenders. I gave them Norah Batty in wrinkled stockings."
John Gregory on working with limited finances at Villa

"The secret of being a good manager is to keep the six players who hate you away from the five who are undecided."
Jock Stein

"The easiest team for a manager to pick is Hindsight XI."

Scotland boss Craig Brown

"My best-ever signing was my wife, Marina."

Celtic manager Kenny Dalglish

"I think we won that game against Liverpool because we scored and they didn't."

Chelsea's Jose Mourinho

"Our draws have been more like victories without goals."

Everton boss Roberto Martinez

"Achilles tendon injuries are the worst you can probably have – they are a pain in the butt."

Leeds manager David O'Leary

"I always enjoy the summer. You can't lose any matches."

Roy Evans

"They said I lost the changing room. I know where it is, it's down the corridor on the left."

Palace manager Ian Holloway

"As one door closes, another one shuts."

Sunderland boss Howard Wilkinson

Can You Manage?

"People say we are having no luck, but we are – it's just all bad."

Boro manager Gareth Southgate

"I always take my notebook into the toilet to sketch out some match situations."

Rangers boss Dick Advocaat

"I've introduced something new to the training. It's called running."

New Spurs manager Gerry Francis

"I've got players here I can't give away!"

Harry Redknapp

FIELD OF DREAMS

"It's been so long since we've had a penalty, nobody knew who was taking it. We had forgotten where the spot was."

Middlesbrough boss Steve McClaren

"Portugal play football as I like to see it played. As a neutral it was fantastic. Unfortunately I'm not a neutral."

Kevin Keegan after Portugal beat England at Euro 2000

"I played so badly that even my parents booed me off when I was substituted."

Theo Walcott for England U21s

"I'll try not to apologise too much for the game
but I'm glad I got in for free."
**Leicester's Micky Adams after a stalemate
with Southampton**

"Their goals were just comedy. You'd probably
win £250 on Candid Camera for that second
one."
**Palace manager Neil Warnock after losing
to Forest**

"We were caviar in the first half, cabbage in the
second."
**Phil Thompson on Liverpool's display at
Charlton**

"The pitch was terrible. The ball was like a rabbit and it's difficult to catch a rabbit."

Rafa Benitez after a Liverpool triumph at Hull

"I was excited and it takes a lot to get me excited – ask my wife."

Roy Keane on a Sunderland win over Spurs

"It was a horrible, horrible debut... I was devastated... it was a long weekend for me. I couldn't even say I could take the dog out for a walk because I haven't got a dog."

Sunderland's Andy Cole after a 7-1 defeat against Everton

"You only have to fart in the box to concede a penalty these days."
Leeds boss Kevin Blackwell on a spot-kick awarded to QPR

"Before my Besiktas debut, they sacrificed a lamb on the pitch and daubed its blood on my forehead for luck. They never did that at QPR."
Les Ferdinand

"Keith Curle has an ankle injury but we'll have to take it on the chin."
Man City manager Alan Ball

"No regrets, none at all. My only regret is that we went out on penalties. That's my only regret. But no, no regrets."

Mick McCarthy after Ireland's 2002 World Cup exit

"They had a dozen corners, maybe 12 – I'm guessing."

Scotland's Craig Brown

"If it smells of sweat in here, it's me. The match was just so exciting!"

Borussia Dortmund boss Jurgen Klopp to Schalke manager Fred Rutten in the lift after a 3-3 draw

Field of Dreams

"I remember swapping jerseys with Franco Baresi. What was depressing was that he got a sweat-soaked Scotland No.9 shirt while the Italy No.6 I got in return was not only bone-dry but still smelling of his cologne."

Ally McCoist

"Joe Cole missed an open goal that my f*cking missus could have scored."

Harry Redknapp

"I am ashamed. I am shocked at the way we played. We played like a bunch of drunks."

Yossi Benayoun after West Ham's 6-0 defeat to Reading

"We must have had 99 per cent of the game. It was the other three per cent that cost us the match."

Chelsea's Ruud Gullit

"When he picked the ball up, I'd be a liar if I said I thought he would score. I thought he was going to head it."

Southampton boss Harry Redknapp on Peter Crouch offering to take a penalty

"I took a whack on my left ankle, but something told me it was my right."

Villa midfielder Lee Hendrie

"He had some curried goat and maybe that was why he was fuelled up today."
Alan Pardew after Papiss Cisse's two goals for Newcastle against Liverpool

"If you took the goals out of it, I think it was pretty even."
Alan Curbishley on West Ham's 4-0 rout by Chelsea

"At least we were consistent – useless in defence, useless in midfield and crap up front."
Ron Atkinson after Aston Villa lost at Coventry

"The only way to stop Henry? With a gun!"

Chelsea's Gianluca Vialli on Thierry Henry

"[Andy] Cole should be scoring from those distances, but I'm not going to single him out."

Alex Ferguson

"When I played for Forest at Derby, they were chucking coins and spitting at me when I took throw-ins. And that was just the old ladies."

Stuart Pearce

"It was the first four goals that cost us the game."

Southampton boss David Jones

"I've only got two words for how we played out there tonight – not good enough."

Newcastle's Sir Bobby Robson

"I regretted not putting myself on the bench after 10 minutes of the game."

Leeds boss Neil Warnock on his first match

"[Loic] Remy looked like he might be getting over that groin strain. He showed a few flashes."

QPR manager Harry Redknapp

"At half-time I would have settled for a corner!"

Leicester's Martin O'Neill

TALKING BALLS

"In six months he said just two words to me, 'You're fired'."

Tomas Brolin on George Graham

"I'd rather buy a Bob the Builder CD for my two-year-old than Roy Keane's book."

Jason McAteer

"If I am so tough, why do my teammates call me Lily?"

Robbie Savage

"If he was a chocolate drop, he'd eat himself."

Archie Gemmill on Graeme Souness

"Ally McCoist is like dog sh*t in the penalty area. You don't know he's there until the damage is done."

John Hughes

"[Jock Stein] just walked up to me and said, 'Right, you are on you fat b*stard'."

Scotland keeper Alan Rough came on for the second half against Wales

"Our new Czech keeper Jan Stejskal only knows three words of English – 'my ball', 'away' and one other."

QPR's Ray Wilkins

"Cloughie called me Edward. I told him I preferred Teddy. He said, 'Right you are, Edward'."

Teddy Sheringham on Brian Clough

"He only has to fart during a warm-up and they're singing his name from the rafters."

Ashley Cole on Freddie Ljungberg

"He was an excellent player, a great defender, but he had the personality of a tennis racket – and I told him so. And he thumped me. It was fair enough I suppose."

Mark Dennis on Southampton manager Chris Nicholl

"John Byrne says his hair is natural. He must be using natural bleach."
Sunderland's Paul Bracewell

"As a player, he was a ranter and a raver. But I think he's taken it back a bit. He's just a ranter now."
Paul McShane on Roy Keane

"He had a first touch like a tackle."
Neville Southall on Brett Angel

"He's a fantastic player. When he isn't drunk."
Brian Laudrup on Paul Gascoigne

"We often played golf together and he always beat me. Then one day I won for the first time. Two weeks later, I was sold."
Chris Nicholl on Villa boss Ron Saunders

"I'm more afraid of my mum than Sven-Goran Eriksson or David Moyes."
Wayne Rooney

"Ninety-five per cent of my problems with the English language are the fault of that stupid little midget."
Gianfranco Zola on Dennis Wise

Sir Alf Ramsay: "I'll be watching you for the first 45 minutes and if you don't work harder, I'll pull you off at half-time."

Rodney Marsh: "Blimey – at Manchester City, all we get is an orange and a cup of tea."

"I went back to the [hotel] room and found Gazza had defecated in my shorts."

John Salako on England duty

"I went in [to see Brian Clough] shaking with fear to ask for a pay rise. I accepted a whisky and a wage cut."

Martin O'Neill

"If Dennis Bergkamp was in Star Trek, he'd be the best player in whatever solar system they were in."

Ian Wright

"When he [Alex Ferguson] starts with the hairdryer treatment on them, I've seen foreign players turn pink and black players turn white."

Rio Ferdinand

"I have got big legs and a big backside – it's just the way I am, I will always have a big a*se. I can't get rid of that."

David Dunn

"Wayne Rooney can go all the way to the top if he keeps his head firmly on the ground."
David Unsworth

"Becks hasn't changed since I've known him. He's always been a flash cockney git."
Ryan Giggs

"I love Kenny [Dalglish]... Very easy to talk to, very hard to understand."
Gary Speed

"I've known him since he was 6ft 3ins!"
Steve Harper on Andy Carroll

THE FUNNIEST FOOTBALL QUOTES... EVER!

BOARDROOM BANTER

"It is like being in a goldfish bowl, as it was when I was a player. As a chairman it's like that, except someone has stuck a blender in there as well. And switched it on."

Niall Quinn at Sunderland

"When I left Leeds I had two options – to jump off the top of a tall building or to cope. I decided to cope."

Peter Ridsdale on taking over at Cardiff

"Roman Abramovich has parked his Russian tank in our front garden and is firing £50 notes at us."

Arsenal chief David Dein

"He uttered the six worst words in the English language: 'I want to play for Liverpool'."
Everton chief Bill Kenwright on Nick Barmby's Reds move

"I'm not going to drag it out or make a point, because points are pointless."
Palace chairman Simon Jordan

"We had a lovely dinner with Kenny, his wife Marina and son Paul. I understood about half of what he said and just nodded when I couldn't understand."
Liverpool chairman Tom Werner on Kenny Dalglish's return as manager

"I liken the current situation to that of the Starship Enterprise. The shields are up and the Klingons are shooting at us and every time they land a punch they are sapping our power."
Southampton's Rupert Lowe

"With Ravanelli and Emerson, perhaps their brains were in their boots and their hearts in their wallets."
Middlesbrough chief Steve Gibson

"Football hooligans? Well, there are the 92 club chairmen for a start."
Brian Clough

"No football-club owner in his right mind would willingly invite an average agent into his academy, any more than a brothel owner would let a syphilitic nutter into his brothel."
Simon Jordan

"Alan Shearer is boring – we call him Mary Poppins. He never gets into trouble."
Newcastle's Freddy Shepherd

"When you shook hands with him, you counted your fingers."
Tommy Docherty on his former QPR chairman Jim Gregory

"In Italy referees are all handsome, athletic, telegenic. Here they have tubby bellies and they blow up very little because they are not mad about getting noticed."
QPR chief Flavio Briatore

"Only women and horses work for nothing."
Villa chairman Doug Ellis on awarding himself a pay rise

"Peter Swales wore a wig, a blazer with an England badge on it and high-heeled shoes. As a man he really impressed me."
Man City manager Malcolm Allison

"I'm not star-struck around players. How could I be? I'm the biggest star here."

Chelsea's Ken Bates

"When I was asked whether I got on with other chairman what I said was, it's fair to say that a fair proportion of them are tossers, but I am pretty sure they think the same thing about me."

Simon Jordan

"Alan Sugar isn't always right you know. Anyone had an Amstrad computer?"

West Ham's David Sullivan

"Our objective is to keep Arsenal English, but with a lot of foreign players."

Peter Hill-Wood

"A few of us want to discuss super leagues but all the rest can talk about is the price of meat pies."

Rangers chief David Murray

"Rather than the super scorer we hoped for, we acquired a super-size, a player devoted to filling his belly more than filling the net."

Karren Brady on her West Ham striker Benni McCarthy

"Well, it's a love-hate relationship – and he loves me."

Villa's Graham Taylor on 'Deadly' Doug Ellis

"We nearly didn't sign him because the letters did not fit on his shirt."

David Dein on Arsenal's signing of Giovanni van Bronckhorst

"If any one ugly b*stard was going to beat us, I'm glad it was you!"

Sunderland's Niall Quinn to Mick McCarthy after a Wolves victory

CALLING THE SHOTS

"[Jurgen] Klinsmann has taken to English football like a duck out of water."

Gerry Francis on the German striker

"Kevin Phillips was so keen to join up with England that he almost got here early enough to meet the last squad going home."

Kevin Keegan

"He has that smell to be where he needs to be at the decisive moment. When there is chocolate to take in the box, he is there."

Arsene Wenger on Julio Baptista

"[Marians] Pahars has also caught every virus going except a computer virus and he is probably working on that even now."
Gordon Strachan on his player's poor fitness record

"Landon [Donovan] said he had the flu. I told him people from Los Angeles don't get flu."
Everton's David Moyes

"The way Ashley Young is built, he looks like a heavy shower could kill him."
Villa boss Martin O'Neill

"Shaun Wright-Phillips has got a big heart. It's as big as him, which isn't very big, but it's bigger."

Man City boss Kevin Keegan

"Mickey [Thomas] gave you everything on the pitch, but there was no real discipline. He even managed to write off a club car in a car wash."

Everton's Howard Kendall

"You're from Drumchapel, laddie. What do you know about prawn cocktails? You'll have a soup like the rest of us."

Jock Stein to Andy Gray on an away trip

"For the first time we have two central defenders who have been pillars and not pillocks."
Bobby Robson on Darren Peacock and Steve Howey

"He is our player. He definitely has attributes. But he is the sort of player that could get me the sack."
Neil Lennon on Georgios Samaras

"We reckon Carlton [Palmer] covers every blade of grass... but then you have to if your first touch is that cr*p."
Dave Jones

"[Enrique] De Lucas' pedigree is unbelievable. If he were a dog, he'd win Crufts."

Ian Holloway on the Blackpool star

"Mario woke up this morning with a hardening – in his thigh!"

Jurgen Klopp on Dortmund star Mario Gotze

"I think he thought he was a Zidane. He wasn't. He was also a very cold fish."

David O'Leary on Harry Kewell

"Where his balls go, you will be quite surprised."

Arsene Wenger on Denilson's attributes

"I haven't seen the lad but he comes highly recommended by my greengrocer."
Brian Clough on buying Nigel Jemson

"I love Kevin Doyle. As a player, not as a man. I love women, without a doubt."
Giovanni Trapattoni

"David Ginola has just handed in a transfer request. The handwriting was beautiful."
Kenny Dalglish

"He had the fattest backside in football at the time."
Walter Smith on Ally McCoist in the 90s

"He's the only man I know who could start an argument with himself."

Sir Bobby Robson on Craig Bellamy

"Once Tony Daley opens his legs, you're in trouble."

Howard Wilkinson

"Tommy Johnson is brainless and talented, which suits our system perfectly."

Neil Warnock on his Notts County striker

"Eric Cantona couldn't tackle a fish supper."

Sir Alex Ferguson

"I've told him there is always room for bald, grumpy old men in my team."

Gordon Strachan on Chris Marsden

"His left foot is so good he could open a jar of pickles with it."

Villa boss John Gregory on Steve Staunton

"Samassi Abou don't speak the English too good."

West Ham manager Harry Redknapp

"I talk to Carra... If you can understand him you can understand anyone."

Rafa Benitez on Jamie Carragher

"I don't like to use the word 'dropped'. He just fell outside the 23."

Roy Hodgson on Ashley Young failing to make the squad

"John Hartson's got more previous than Jack the Ripper."

Harry Redknapp on John Hartson

"I've just introduced Nigel Martyn to a clean sheet. The last time he had one Kenneth Wolstenholme was the commentator."

Palace boss Steve Coppell

"He dribbled through Spurs' defence like Ricky Villa, but his finish was more like Ricky Gervais."
Liverpool manager Brendan Rodgers on Raheem Sterling

"He just needs to make his brain work. That is his only problem."
Roberto Mancini to Mario Balotelli

"If he was an inch taller he'd be the best centre half in Britain. His father is 6ft 2in – I'd check the milkman."
Sir Alex Ferguson on Gary Neville

THE FUNNIEST FOOTBALL QUOTES... EVER!

OFF THE PITCH

Q: "What's your best advice to young players?"

Gerry Taggart: "Drink lots of beer and smoke loads of fags."

"I've never had a drink, never, not once. I'm teetotal. The girlfriend does, mind, she drinks for us both."

Leeds striker Alan Smith

"My wife said to me in bed, 'God, your feet are cold'. I said, 'You can call me Brian in bed, dear'."

Brian Clough on married life

"I don't see how one kebab can be the difference between beating one or three men or running from box to box or scoring a goal."
Paul Gascoigne is confused about being left out of England's World Cup squad

"The man who comes to take care of my piranhas tells me he will kill all my fish if I leave West Ham."
Paolo Di Canio

"It took a lot of bottle for Tony Adams to own up to his drink problem."
Ian Wright

"After you've signed at Celtic, the first thing you're told is where it's best not to go to refuel your car!"

Jan Vennegoor of Hesselink

"Sven's a lucky man with the ladies. In fact, he's very lucky because, with respect, he's no Brad Pitt."

Martin O'Neill on the England manager

"If it wasn't for Tracey, I'd be an 18-stone bricklayer playing for Penicuik Athletic."

Andy Goram on his wife

"I was recognised too much [in Liverpool] and sometimes women would suddenly climb all over me."
Everton's Marouane Fellaini

"I just shook hands with him. Imagine how many boobs that hand's touched."
Paul Gascoigne on meeting Sean Connery

Head waiter: "Mr Allison, your bar bill – I have to tell you, it is enormous."
Malcolm Allison: "Is that all? You insult me. Don't come back until it's double that!"

"Life's tough. I've had to swap my Merc for a BMW, I'm down to my last 37 suits and I'm drinking non-vintage champagne."

Ron Atkinson after being fired by United

"I have discovered Newcastle Brown Ale and my ambition is to speak Geordie as well as Peter Beardsley."

David Ginola

"When I said I had no regrets, I'd forgotten about that haircut and it has come back to haunt me on several occasions."

Everton's Trevor Steven

"If they made a film of my life, I think they should get George Clooney to play me. He's a fantastic actor and my wife thinks he would be ideal."

Chelsea boss Jose Mourinho

"In 1969 I gave up women and alcohol. It was the worst 20 minutes of my life."

George Best

"Dennis Wise grabbed my tit. I had five finger marks around the nipple, like a love bite. That took some explaining to the missus."

Liverpool's Jason McAteer

Q: "What would you have done if you hadn't been a footballer?"

A: "A funeral director. I like looking at dead bodies."

Chris Sutton

"I took my wife out on Saturday night but all I was thinking about was our back four. It was like taking the back four out as well."

Sunderland manager Roy Keane

"I'll have it in four, I would never eat eight."

Jason McAteer on how many slices he likes his pizza cut into

"I'll tell you what my dream is. I mean my absolute number one dream that I will die happy if it happens – I want to see a UFO."
Paul Gascoigne

"[Curtis Fleming] is teaching me how to speak a bit of Irish and drink Guinness. I'm struggling. I only really know how to drink Guinness."
Ireland striker Clinton Morrison

"Liverpool is such a beautiful city, with a lot of culture – and I love living here. I have even learned how to cook spaghetti and fried eggs."
Everton's Li Wei Feng

"The lifestyle is much the same – bad clothing, bad food – so we don't expect too much."

Alf-Inge Haaland explains why Norwegians adapt so well to England

"It's not nice going to the supermarket and the woman at the till thinking, 'Dodgy keeper'."

Liverpool goalie David James

"If there's anyone luckier than a footballer, it's a footballer's wife. She has all the money and prestige but none of the pressure."

Gordon Strachan's view on WAGs

"I did a 24-hour sponsored silence for Children In Need and if I hadn't had my girlfriend to talk to, I think I would have struggled."
Sunderland's Anton Ferdinand

"I blew the lot on vodka and tonic, gambling and fags. Looking back, I think I overdid it on the tonic."
Ex-QPR forward Stan Bowles

"The cook prepares very good food. I prefer to stay here and eat rather than going to my house. But don't tell my wife."
West Ham's Gianfranco Zola

THE FUNNIEST FOOTBALL QUOTES... EVER!

REF
JUSTICE

"The referee made three mistakes only. The red card, playing too much time at the end of the first half and the penalty. Apart from that he was good."

Chelsea boss Avram Grant

"I don't want to complain about the referee but it did appear a jittery and nervous performance."

Reading manager Steve Coppell

"The ref was a big-time homer, more interested in his rub-on suntan."

Everton's David Moyes on Jeff Winter

"The linesman, he'll watch it tonight, when his wife's making him a bacon sandwich and he'll think, 'F*ck me what have I done there today?'"
Spurs boss Harry Redknapp

"If that's a penalty, then I may as well say I'm Alec McJockstrap and wear a kilt."
Leicester manager Ian Holloway

"[Marcus Merk] is always against us. He must have been let out of prison to referee this match."
Jose Mourinho after Porto's clash with Deportivo La Coruna

"The referee must have felt like the President of the United States at the time of the Cuban missile crisis."
Howard Wilkinson after Leeds' game was postponed due to a waterlogged pitch

"It's like a toaster, the ref's shirt pocket. Every time there's a tackle, up pops a yellow card."
Man City boss Kevin Keegan

"I'd like to smash the ball into a referee at 200mph and see if he can get out of the way."
Sir Bobby Robson on Nolberto Solano's red card for hand ball

"I tried to talk to the ref but it's easier to get an audience with the Pope. If I'm in London again and I get mugged, I hope the same amount of people turn up. There were six police officers, four stewards and a UN peace-keeping observer."

Gordon Strachan after Southampton lost to Arsenal

"I don't think we should have shoot-outs. We should have a shoot-the-ref shoot-out. After that penalty, the referee should have been shot."

John Gregory after Villa gave away a late penalty in a cup shoot-out defeat

"The referee told me this was his last match before he retired and maybe he wanted to go out with a bang. I just wish he'd retired before today."
Southampton manager Dave Jones on the official Gerald Ashby

"The referee was booking so many people I thought he was filling in his lottery numbers."
Arsenal striker Ian Wright

"I'm just glad the referees can't understand what he's saying to them."
Everton's Joe Royle on Duncan Ferguson

"Referees should be wired up to a couple of electrodes. They should be allowed three mistakes – then you run 50,000 volts through their genitals."
Aston Villa's John Gregory

"I thanked the referee for giving us three cracking throw-ins, even when one of them might have been their ball."
Notts County boss Neil Warnock

"I think if the referee had stood still, we wouldn't have chased him."
Man United's Roy Keane on Andy D'Urso

"No doubt the ref will have gone down the pub, boasted to his mates that he sent off Neil Ruddock and felt proud of himself."
Palace defender Neil Ruddock

"If the referee stands by that decision, I have two wooden legs. I will be seeing this ref again in my dreams – and I won't be kissing him!"
Leicester boss Ian Holloway after skipper Patrick Kisnorbo was sent off

"Of the nine red cards this season we probably deserved half of them."
Arsenal boss Arsene Wenger

"Maybe I scored a goal against his favourite team 30 years ago."
Celtic manager Gordon Strachan on referee Stuart Dougal who sent him to the stands

"In England, the referees either shoot you down with a machine gun or don't blow their whistle at all."
Chelsea's Gianluca Vialli

"The referee was bobbins. If you need that translating, it means cr*p."
Southampton manager Dave Jones

"I behaved like a monkey out there. I went too far."

Borussia Dortmund boss Jurgen Klopp reflects on being sent to the stands

"Can anyone tell me why they give referees a watch? It's certainly not for keeping the time."

Sir Alex Ferguson on Graham Poll who added just three minutes of stoppage time

"How can women referees make accurate decisions if they have never been tackled from behind by a 14-stone centre half, elbowed in the ribs, or even caught offside?"

Man City manager Joe Royle

"Yes I did receive a two-match ban for calling a ref Coco the Clown but I'm down to one after today."
Newcastle boss Joe Kinnear

"Yes, I swear a lot. But the advantage is that having played abroad I can choose a different language from the referee's."
Tottenham striker Jurgen Klinsmann

"What is the point of talking to him, he's one of the most arrogant men I have met."
Leicester boss Nigel Pearson when asked if he would speak to the referee after the game

GAME FOR A LAUGH

"I've never wanted to leave. I'm here for the rest of my life, and hopefully after that as well."
Mark Schwarzer

"If I had not been a footballer, I would have been a doctor, or porn star."
Christian Karembeu

"The last time I lifted a weight? Probably that can of Red Bull the other day."
Jamie Vardy

"I've been consistent in patches this season."
Arsenal winger Theo Walcott

"If I played for Scotland my grandma would
be the proudest woman in the country, if she
wasn't dead."
Mark Crossley

"I was terrified on my first day. I had only
just passed my driving test too, so getting to
Leicester was a big nervous affair in itself!"
Alan Smith on joining Leicester

"I don't know if Alex McLeish knows whether
I'm Scottish or not. Maybe I'll have to put 'Mac'
in front of my surname."
Chris Iwelumo

"I remember the game because I managed to do something very few players can claim – I set up an international goal for Brian McClair!"
Ally McCoist recalls his 50th cap

"My wife said I looked good in hoops. After QPR there weren't that many options."
Marc Bircham on joining Yeovil, who wear green and white hoops

"Last year I had a foot operation. Then my thigh went. This season I'm going to play it by ear."
John Aldridge

"We are happy with three points, but it could have been more."
Ryan Giggs

"As England goalkeeper you are always there to be shot at."
Paul Robinson

"My father was a footballer – he only ate peas because they were round."
Fabricio Coloccini

"My ankle injury's been a real pain in the a*se."
David Prutton

"Leeds is a great club and it's been my home for years, even though I live in Middlesbrough."
Jonathan Woodgate

"Even if there is one game to go and we are 12 points behind, we'll still believe."
Joe Hart

"I'm as happy as I can be – but I have been happier."
Ugo Ehiogu

"I can see the carrot at the end of the tunnel."
Stuart Pearce

"I've been training for just over a month now but for the first two weeks of that I couldn't even catch flu."
Antti Niemi

"I'd like to play for an Italian club like Barcelona."
Mark Draper

"My eyes water when they sing 'You'll Never Walk Alone'. I've actually been crying while playing."
Kevin Keegan

"My mum would kill me if I wore gloves in a game."
Matt Jarvis

"I would not be bothered if we lost every game as long as we won the league."

Mark Viduka

"[Being a footballer] is the best job in the world. The second best is being a footballer's wife."

Gary McAllister

"I'm very passionate about antiques because they are like people."

Emmanuel Petit

"It's great to get that duck off my back."

Gary Cahill

"I've never been so certain about anything in my life. I want to be a coach. Or a manager. I'm not sure which."
Phil Neville

"Rangers fans were friendly to me. The most hostility I got was being pelted with snowballs when I went to take a corner at Aberdeen."
Stiliyan Petrov

"When I scored my first goal for England, I was so excited I didn't know what to do or where to run. David [Beckham] just pointed and said, 'The England fans are that way, mate'."
Wayne Rooney

THE FUNNIEST FOOTBALL QUOTES... EVER!

MEDIA CIRCUS

Journalist: "Expecting any action, Gordon?"

Gordon Strachan: "You'd better ask my wife."

The manager when asked about transfers

"The English press are a very nice bunch of b*stards."

Graham Taylor

"True fame is when the newspapers spell your name right in Karachi."

Brian Clough

Reporter: "I'm from the Sun."

Paul Gascoigne: "I'm from the earth."

"In his interviews, [David] Beckham manages to sit on the fence very well and keeps both ears on the ground."
Ireland manager Brian Kerr

"What other way would you approach a game? Must-lose? Must-draw?"
Roy Keane when asked by a reporter if it was a "must-win game"

Journalist: "What's it like to go from zero to hero?"
Celtic's Lubo Moravcik to his interpreter: "Tell him I was never a zero."

"I am dilly ding, dilly dong. I am a bell, haha. Don't write, 'Ranieri is a bell'. Hey, hey!"

Leicester boss Claudio Ranieri

Reporter: "Why did you take Jack Wilshere off?"

Wenger: "It was 9.25, past his bedtime."

Wilshere was then aged just 16

"Will you stop playing with yourself when you are talking to me, it's rude!"

Gordon Strachan to a TV reporter nervously jangling coins in his pocket during a post-match interview

"The press in England make from a little mosquito a big elephant."
Chelsea's Ruud Gullit

"It's not that he doesn't like the press. It's just that he doesn't like talking to them."
Joe Royle on Duncan Ferguson refusing to speak to the media

"I look a little bit like a serial killer, but you [the reporter] have ones like that too so you are used to it."
Jurgen Klopp when asked if he was sporting new glasses after losing his last pair

"Do you fancy me or something?"

David Beckham after a male journalist asked about his latest haircut

"You're welcome to my phone number, gentlemen, but please remember not to ring me during The Sweeney."

Ron Atkinson on his first day as Man United manager

"You'll have to excuse me, I keep burping. I've had a glass of beer."

Alan Pardew apologises to the press after a Newcastle win against Stoke

"You guys probably write the truth. Then in the office the editors chop out the important things. Like facts."
Kevin Keegan

"No comment, lads – and that's off the record."
Ally McCoist to a group of reporters during a Rangers media ban

"Since coming to Celtic a few months ago, the newspapers have linked me with 210 players. Fair enough, but some of those mentioned I am not interested in, some I've never heard of and two of them are dead."
Martin O'Neill

Journalist: "Do Forest have a chance of staying up?"

Ron Atkinson: "Did you ask the captain of the Titanic the same question?"

"Just tell them I completely disagree with everything they say!"

Bill Shankly to a translator when being surrounded by rowdy Italian journalists

Brazilian reporter: "What do you think of Brazil?"

Kenny Dalglish: "I think he's a great player."

The forward at the 1982 World Cup

"We don't have reporters any more – we have QCs. Nowadays they aren't interested in how many goals a player scores, but where he's scoring at night."
Joe Royle

"Football journalists? They're just about able to do joined-up writing."
Sir Alan Sugar

"Can we go now please? I'd like a beer."
Jack Charlton to the media after Ireland's 3-0 loss to Portugal

THE FUNNIEST FOOTBALL QUOTES... EVER!

Printed in Great Britain
by Amazon

13059177R00061